C. S. Lewis's Cambridge

A Walking Tour Guide

by

Jacqueline Glenny

Published by
Christian Heritage Press
Round Church Vestry
Bridge Street
Cambridge
CB2 1UB

Email: admin@christianheritageuk.org.uk
Website: www.christianheritageuk.org.uk

Christian Heritage Press is a division of Christian Heritage, Cambridge which is committed to demonstrating to our modern global society that Christianity is a living faith with the power to change people and therefore to shape history.

Design and production by Stephen Lown **Graphic Designer**
Photographs © Magdalene College, Jacqueline J. Glenny and Martin Lown

ISBN 0-9541762-1-9

Foreword

C. S. Lewis was clearly very happy during his time at Cambridge but I am so glad he was still in Oxford when I was a student there, reading English in the late 1940s. I had already heard about him before I went up. My uncle, who was at Oxford in the 1920s, knew him and had belonged to a theological discussion group with him before Lewis's conversion, and my father also had met him and encouraged him after his early book, 'The Pilgrim's Regress', had suffered from unfavourable reviews.

I also vividly remember, as a teenager living in the country during the Second World War, rushing home from Sunday School to hear his broadcast talks – later to be published in 'Mere Christianity'. As Jacqueline Glenny says in this helpful account, one of his greatest strengths as a speaker was that of making things clear, so that for young Christians like me it was encouraging to hear the faith logically and reasonably presented on the wireless.

One of the chief attractions of Oxford for me, therefore, was the fact that C. S. Lewis was there. He was, undoubtedly, one of the two best teachers I have ever had. Though I did not have the privilege of having one-to-one tutorials with him, I can warmly endorse everything that Professor Glenny says about him as a lecturer. He did not really like us to take notes in his lectures, preferring us to listen as he spoke and then go back to our rooms and make notes on whatever we had heard. And his clarity was such that we remembered. Sometimes I fear that the concentration in recent years on his marriage and his loss has overshadowed his supreme mastery as a teacher of literature as well as of Christian and ethical subjects. Professor Glenny is right to refer to the breadth and depth of his literary repertoire.

As a footnote, shortly before Professor Lewis died, our son, aged seven, wrote to him enthusing about the Narnia books. He got an answer, almost by return of post, thanking him for his letter and encouraging him to read E. Nesbit as well.

Many people throughout the world are grateful to C. S. Lewis, Professor of Literature and Christian apologist. Cambridge was honoured to have him for nine years.

Lady Elizabeth Catherwood
September 2003

Preface

I spent four months in Cambridge researching C. S. Lewis's Cambridge years. I wanted to discover the city where Lewis spent most of his final nine years of life. One of the delights of my time in Cambridge was to go on walking tours led by guides who provided historical insight into the city. During the walks I also had an opportunity to meet people who came from all over the world to visit Cambridge.

On a tour one Tuesday afternoon in March, I met Barbara, an enthusiastic woman from New Jersey. When I told her that I was doing some biographical research on Clive Staples Lewis's life in Cambridge, she reacted immediately and probed, 'What years would Lewis have been here?'

I explained, 'He moved to Cambridge in January of 1955 and left when he resigned his position in the late summer of 1963. His weekdays were spent here in Cambridge and the weekends and break times at his Oxford home, The Kilns.'

At this Barbara paused and then excitedly remarked, 'I knew Lewis had been in Cambridge sometime during his life, but I always thought that it was his early years. Most people seem to associate Lewis with Oxford University. I just never got around to checking out the dates of Lewis's Cambridge years.'

She continued, 'I must tell you why I am so interested in the dates. When I was ten years old, my family moved to Cambridge for a year during my father's sabbatical at the Cavendish Laboratory. We lived in a house on Emmanuel Road near the bus station. Across the street from the house is Christ's Pieces, a large open public park and walking area.

'After school I would often go across the street to play by myself. I was especially attracted to a huge tree stump with a deep, large cavity. The inside had rotted away so that I could sit in it and my head would still be below the cut line. I loved to pretend that I was invisible to the world in my little house where I spent hours reading or telling myself stories out loud.

'One day in the late autumn of 1958 while playing in my tree stump, I was suddenly aware of a person towering above me. My banter was silenced when the large, looming backside of a man claimed a few inches of the stump as a stool.

'I held my breath and froze motionless. I then heard a rich, spellbinding voice launching into a story. To this day I don't remember the story, but I cannot get the fascinating experience out of my mind. After what seemed like ten minutes, the portly figure, as quietly and quickly as he appeared, stood to resume his walk, without giving a hint that he had seen me.

'Astonished, I scrambled up and I peeked my head out just enough to watch the man walk slowly away. He seemed purposely to choose an angle that allowed me to see the side of his face, which I locked in my memory with the hope of future sightings. He never made direct eye contact with me, but a smile played about his lips. You could see his eyes were alive with satisfaction over the shared pleasure.

'During the rest of my time in Cambridge, I always looked for my storytelling friend, hoping to find him and to pull another tale from him. His face was fixed in my mind, but to my disappointment I never saw him again at Christ's Pieces or on the streets of Cambridge before I moved.

'As a girl of fourteen living back in the States, I saw a picture of C. S. Lewis. I was amazed. I had seen this man before! This was the man who entered my make-believe, invisible childhood world on a late fall afternoon when I lived in Cambridge. Yet, I dismissed this possibility. It surely could not have been Lewis; he was a man who just happened to look like him. I assumed that Lewis only spent a few of his early years in Cambridge and that his final years were at Oxford, for Oxford is the city usually mentioned when referring to Lewis.'

Barbara looked at me and said, 'You have confirmed what I have always dreamed: that it was possible for C. S. Lewis to have offered a child the gift of his imagination for a few moments on a weekday afternoon.'

It is my wish that you also may encounter the spirit of C. S. Lewis as you walk the streets of Cambridge where he once walked.

Jacqueline Glenny

A Walking Tour of C. S. Lewis's Cambridge

Welcome to Cambridge! You will find present-day Cambridge a charming, bustling city with a varied population of students, academics and townspeople engaged in their daily activities. However, it will not take you long to discover that the streets of Cambridge echo with the footsteps of notable people who have spent time in this city.

The rich history of Cambridge demonstrates why this city has been the destination of thousands, including the Romans, spiritual leaders, scholars and royalty. From the thirteenth century, Cambridge has been among the greatest centres of knowledge in the world. Cambridge University was the attraction that drew C. S. Lewis to spend the final years of his life here.

Suggestions

Wear good comfortable walking shoes. Bring an umbrella for the weather can be unpredictable. The historic centre of town is about one mile long and half a mile wide. Other interesting sites not related to C. S. Lewis will be referred to along the way for you to explore or note for a return visit.

Start this walking tour, if possible, to coincide with the hours of the colleges in Cambridge. Depending on the time of the academic year, the colleges may or may not be open. The colleges normally can be visited during the Cambridge terms which are **Michaelmas** (October to December), **Lent** (January to mid-March), and **Easter** (from late April to June). Most colleges are closed between terms and from mid-May until mid-June for examinations.

Notice the postings at the gatehouses of the colleges for further information on visitors' hours. Some colleges do charge a small entrance fee, a worthy investment, to walk through their grounds. Cambridge University is a self-governing institution with thirty-one private colleges. Thus, because the colleges are not public property, visitors to the colleges are advised to respect the posted hours when the college is open to the public. Also, do not to walk on the grass; this privilege is reserved for senior members of the colleges.

Evensong services, which are held by many of the colleges in central Cambridge, are open to the public without charge. These services provide an occasion to reflect quietly at the end of the day in a reverential atmosphere of sacred music, scripture readings and splendid architecture. King's College has Choral Evensong at 17:30 on Tuesday-Saturday during term time. Other colleges have services as posted.

Magdalene College, where Lewis resided during his Cambridge years, is open daily from 9:00 – 18:30, except mid-April to mid-June. The renowned **Pepys Library** is open to the public on Monday – Saturday during term from 14:30 – 15:30 and Easter Term and until the end of August from 11:30 – 12:30 as well. The **Fellows' Garden** is open 13:30 – 18:30.

In the Porter's Lodge, ***Magdalene Described***, a useful guide, is available for sale. Though many rooms are not open to the public, you can readily see the layout of the college where Lewis lived and absorb the atmosphere of his academic setting.

While Lewis enjoyed good health, he would arm himself with a map of Cambridge and the surrounding region and explore the area by way of the numerous footpaths. The thematic thread of solitary walks in nature is interwoven in the fibre of Lewis's life. One of Lewis's greatest pleasures was an annual walking tour in Ireland or Wales. He also loved the pleasure of walking in his locale.

The pleasurable communion that Lewis had with nature is evidenced in his life and in his faith. His writings abound with descriptive passages of nature and symbolic meaning. In ***The Chronicles of Narnia***, for example, the coming of Aslan and of Spring point to redemption and hope.

Today, you will find many guidebooks and maps in local bookshops that will direct you to various sights. Enjoy your walk and exploration. Cambridge is a city that will captivate you.

C. S. Lewis and Cambridge University

Clive Staples Lewis, the storyteller, apologist, writer, lecturer, preacher and radio broadcaster, is usually associated with Oxford. However, the last nine years of his life (1954-1963) were spent as a Cambridge University don. The significance of this time cannot be minimized.

During these years Jack Lewis, the name used by his friends in addressing him, became friends with Joy Davidman Gresham. This friendship led to a civil marriage ceremony on 23 April 1956, which was a purely legal act to allow the American woman to remain in England. A second religious ceremony was observed to sanction their marriage on 21 March 1957.

Watching his wife across an Oxford college quadrangle (the open spaces are called courts in Cambridge), Lewis confided to friend Nevill Coghill that he had never expected in his sixties to enjoy the happiness that had passed him by in his twenties.[1]

During this breath of happiness, friends detected a difference in Lewis. His marriage to Joy brought out the more gentle, compassionate side of him. While the relationship between Joy and Jack Lewis was at first glance a seeming irony – in light of Joy's more aggressive personality and Jack's bent toward courtly romanticism – it worked quite well. Lewis, ever the man's man, admired the pluck and intellectual stimulation of this Joy who never ceased to surprise him. Shortly after Lewis moved to Cambridge, it was Joy who inspired him to write one of his more notable fictional pieces, ***Till We Have Faces.***

Magdalene College

Begin your walk at **Magdalene College** (left), which is located where Madgalene Street crosses the River Cam. C. S. Lewis spent almost thirty years of his academic life in Oxford. The move from Magdalen College in Oxford to Magdalene

College (both colleges are pronounced Maudlin – note the final 'e' on the Cambridge version), where Lewis spent the last nine years of his life, was as dramatic and significant as the marriage of Lewis and Joy.[2]

Lewis arrived in Oxford in the spring of 1917 where his undergraduate work was done at University College. He was awarded a scholarship to read Classics. The war, however, interrupted his education. Lewis enlisted in the Army in the summer of 1917 and spent time in France and Germany. Early in 1919 Lewis returned to his college and excelled in Classics, Philosophy and Ancient History.

In the autumn of 1924, Lewis began his first job at Oxford's University College where he had been an undergraduate. In May 1925 he was elected to a fellowship in English at Magdalen College, Oxford (left).

Lewis acknowledged his conversion to theism in the Trinity Term of 1929. Two years later, in September 1931, he embraced faith in Christ. In his autobiography **Surprised by Joy**, Lewis described his mental struggle leading to the

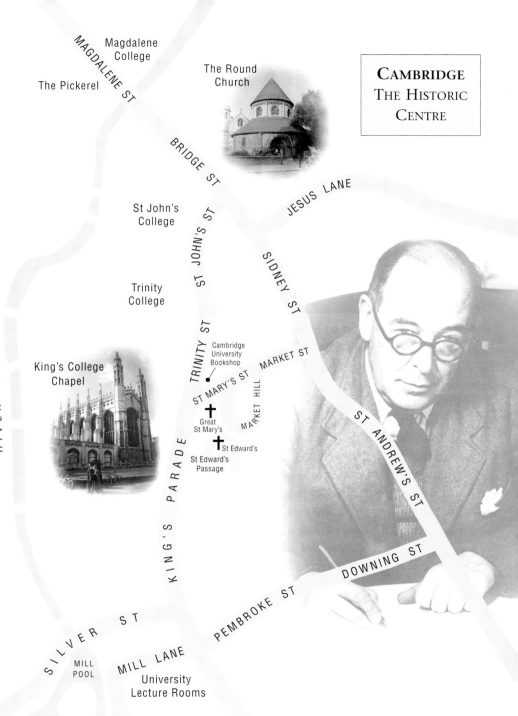

Magdalene
College

MAGDALENE ST

The Pickerel

The Round
Church

BRIDGE ST

JESUS LANE

St John's
College

ST JOHN'S ST

SIDNEY ST

Trinity
College

TRINITY ST

Cambridge
University
Bookshop

MARKET ST

King's College
Chapel

ST MARY'S ST

MARKET HILL

Great
St Mary's

St Edward's

St Edward's
Passage

KING'S PARADE

ST ANDREW'S ST

RIVER

DOWNING ST

SILVER ST

MILL
POOL

MILL LANE

PEMBROKE ST

University
Lecture Rooms

7

point when he chose to accept the truth of Christ's redemptive death and acknowledged the contribution of Christianity to his life.

Lewis had purchased a home four miles from the centre of Oxford – The Kilns (below) in Headington Quarry – in 1930. He also had rooms at Oxford's Magdalen College (Room 3 on Staircase 3 in the New

Buildings), which served him during the week.

Twice at Oxford University Lewis had been passed over for promotion to professor when both the Merton Professor of English Language and Literature and the Goldsmith's Chair of English Literature at New College were vacant. Campaigns against him seemed to be based upon the perception that a professor of English should not win acclaim as an amateur theologian.

No doubt a bit of jealousy was also involved because of Lewis's wide-reaching fame and the resulting attention. During the war, Americans often sent him generous care packages, while most English endured the strict rationing of many food items such as meat and sugar. According to Lewis's good friend and colleague J. R. R. Tolkien, while not a resentful person, Lewis was disheartened by Oxford's ill treatment and began to open his mind to other possibilities.

Cambridge University was not concerned about Lewis's religious ties. On 18 January 1954, the Council of the Senate of Cambridge University announced the need for a Professor in Medieval and Renaissance English, and the chair was advertised on 31 March. Tolkien, one of the three electors of this new chair, was influential in supporting Lewis as the choice for the position.

In May of the same year, Lewis was contacted by the Vice-Chancellor Sir Henry Willink to inform him that the decision to elect Lewis to the chair was 'unanimous with a warmth and sincerity which could not have been exceeded'.[3]

Initially, Lewis rejected the position due to domestic obstacles: he owned a house near Oxford, and he cared for his brother Warren, who suffered from bouts of alcoholism. He was not interested in transferring his entire household to Cambridge.

The prospect of a shift from Oxford to Cambridge was nevertheless appealing to Lewis from the social and academic viewpoints. However, hesitation by Lewis resulted in the position being offered to another candidate.

When the second candidate declined the Cambridge offer, Tolkien strongly urged Lewis to reconsider. Lewis accepted the Chair of Medieval and Renaissance English at Cambridge with the understanding that he would be in Cambridge four days a week in term time and possibly more during exam times. Spending vacations and weekends at The Kilns seemed a workable solution for Lewis, who had lived under a similar arrangement while at Magdalen College in Oxford.

Lewis acknowledged in his letter to Sir Henry Willink, who was coincidentally both Master (President) of Magdalene and Vice-Chancellor of Cambridge University, that the area of great concern was the 'question of rooms in Cambridge (could the College supply me with them?). I could manage well. I can both work and sleep in trains so that the prospect of spending much of my life on the Bletchley route does not alarm me.'[4]

In those days, there was a direct train route between Oxford and Cambridge – a three-hour trip on the 'Cantab Crawler'. The slow train ride was a blessing to Lewis for it often meant he was the sole occupant of a compartment. Lewis usually travelled first class and used the time to read, pray, or enjoy the scenery. Many times, however, particularly at the end or beginning of a term, Lewis hired his Oxford friend Clifford Morris to drive him. They often stopped at a pub or enjoyed a country picnic along the way.

Lewis began his Cambridge duties as Professor of Medieval and Renaissance English in January 1955. The scope of the position challenged him – he would deliver lectures and have more time to write. A comforting thought to Lewis was that his address would still be at 'Magdalene', so he would continue under the same patroness. Nevertheless, Jack and his brother Warren referred to Oxford's Magdalen College as 'The Impenitent' after the move to Cambridge.

Cambridge's Magdalene was quite different from Oxford's Magdalen in several ways. Lewis pronounced that the 'prospect (socially and academically considered) of migrating from Oxford to Cambridge would be more an incentive than a deterrent'.[5]

Cambridge was much more accepting of Lewis, the amateur theologian. Lewis declared his move to Cambridge a grand success. In a letter to an American friend, Lewis wrote,

> I think I shall like Magdalene better than Magdalen. It's a tiny college (a perfect cameo architecturally), and they're all so old fashioned, and pious, and gentle, and conservative – unlike this leftist, atheist, cynical, hardboiled, huge Magdalen.[6]

The softer, more gracious attitude of the town and the college invigorated him and made him feel younger. The fellows of his new college were friendly, a bit more informal and respectfully courteous.

Lewis compared the welcoming environment of Magdalene to a sunlit wall in a familiar garden. John Walsh, former fellow of Magdalene later associated with Jesus College, Oxford, remembered

> Magdalene of my time as more akin to the Cambridge of the Edwardians than that of the meritocratic 1990s. It was relaxed, friendly and easy-going. It was far from being an intellectual hothouse. Among the older dons professionalism in scholarship was respected rather than prized. Cultivation and charm were rated highly. *Belles lettres* were at least as important as tomes.[7]

The First Court

As you pass through the **Gatehouse of Magdalene** you will walk past the **Porter's Lodge** (left). Pause as you enter the **First Court** (right), a small medieval courtyard that reflects the early days of the college when Benedictine monks founded Magdalene College in the 1400s. To the left (north) on ground level is the **Parlour** (the three ground-floor windows from the corner). A small doorway is between the

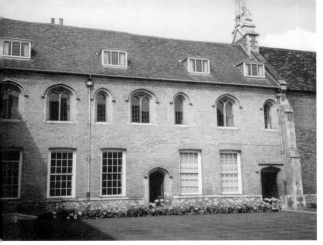

Parlour and the **Old Library**. You will then see a small passageway that leads to the doors of the **Old Library** on the left and the **Chapel** on the right.

Lewis's Rooms

The rooms occupied by Lewis are the five windows above the **Parlour** and the **Old Library**. They are now divided into two offices and are not open to the public. Jack Lewis was offered an academic position through Cambridge University; however, living accommodations were usually arranged independently through the various colleges. Lewis was delighted to be offered a Fellowship at Magdalene, which included a set of rooms.

The one concern that Lewis expressed in a letter to Sir Henry Willink about the rooms was that the 'inches of bookshelf space is the important factor'. Sir Henry wrote to Lewis to inform him there was an 'attractive set of rooms available – two sitting rooms plus bedroom, bath, etc. in the First Court'. Lewis would be offered all the 'social rights of a Fellow' which included rooms and dining in Hall.[8]

The academic tradition of colleges was to provide a set of rooms that served as both living quarters and an academic space to receive students. The university model was based upon the premise that bachelor fellows did not use offices but rather lived in rooms. Their academic endeavours were carried out in a setting that did not compartmentalize social and professional life – they were one – using the monastic model as a basis for academic life.

The students with whom he conducted one-to-one tutorials visited the Oxford rooms of Jack Lewis frequently. His duties at Cambridge would not include tutoring but rather would focus on one or two weekly lectures. He delighted in the opportunity to wake up in Cambridge and decide what he would *like to do* instead of what *must he do*. Lewis declared that the advantage of the Cambridge position was half the work for three times the pay. Nevertheless, while he had tired of tutoring after twenty-nine years, he did find delight in teaching because he could claim so many friends who were younger.[9]

Those who knew him have described Lewis in many ways. Physically, he was heavy-set with a round, red face that boasted twinkling eyes and a wry smile. Former student and Cambridge University colleague George Watson said that Lewis seemed more like a pork butcher with a hearty disposition and large, booming voice. Lewis wore clothing that was rumpled; his chauffeur said he had the distinct ability to make a new set of clothes look shabby by the second wearing. He enjoyed privacy, monotony and solitary nature walks.

Socially, Lewis was exceedingly courteous and able to make conversation as readily with lorry drivers and farmers as with notable Oxbridge minds. He was generally kind and tolerant with all people, except those he perceived as proud. While he was somewhat impatient with children, probably due largely to his limited contact with them, Lewis was very prone to childish delight in storytelling, imagination and adventure.

Lewis enjoyed gatherings of friends at pubs or for after-dinner conversation where he entertained with his jovial storytelling and witty imagination. Even in the last five years of his life, Lewis would refer to some people as being 'grownup' implying that he himself identified with being a 'child' in imaginative thoughts and behaviour.

Once while Lewis was on a walk in the countryside with Simon Barrington-Ward, the Dean of Chapel at Magdalene College, they came upon a farmer working in a field of haystacks. The lengthening shadows cast by the late afternoon sun gave the illusion of a man who was larger than life. Lewis exclaimed, 'Giants have come! Let's go to the village and warn the people.'

Mentally, Jack Lewis was brilliant in conversation, commanding in wit, and formidable in argument. What he had lacked as a child in athletic ability, he compensated for with mental agility that he exercised in verbal jousts, rarely losing a battle. Bishop Barrington-Ward recalled memories of Lewis in a commemorative sermon delivered at Magdalene Chapel after Lewis's death. Lewis's quick mind was combative and yet, at the same time, if you stepped aside from the conflict and simply offered him some tentative idea of your own, he could snatch it up like a favour and whirl it around on his lance until it became a positive banner. Gradually I came to enjoy the nightly entertainment of his marvellous talk, which his writings still so poignantly recall, the rich storehouse of his reading and his skill in drawing aptly upon it.[10]

Constantly, Lewis was called a 'bookish' man who loved books and their ideas. He treated people with equity regardless of age, status, or intellectual ability. Yet, he could give the distinct impression that he was more interested in the ideas a person raised rather than the person.

Lewis possessed an astonishing memory. Many said he read everything and remembered everything he read. One of Lewis's Oxford students described his teacher's ability to hear a line of a poem quoted by a friend or student and then go on and finish quoting the rest of the page.

Kenneth Tynan, Lewis's student, recalled an after-dinner game that Lewis would play in his rooms at Oxford. Lewis asked Tynan to choose a number from one to forty. Once the number was selected, Tynan was told to go to that shelf in the library. Another number between one and twenty was called for. That number was linked to the corresponding book on that shelf, for example, book fifteen. Again, Lewis called for a number. This time it was to be between one and a hundred. For example, if number forty-five were chosen, Tynan was told to turn to page 45 and to pick one further number between one and twenty-five to pinpoint a particular line on the page. For instance, if number seven were selected, Lewis would ask for that line to be read aloud. Lewis would then cite the work, the author and quite frequently finish quoting the remainder of the page.[11]

Once Lewis was married, Joy would make trips to Cambridge to stay for a few days while she helped him with projects or hosted small parties for his friends. Guests at these occasions remembered Joy as being a frail figure due to her fight with cancer, a wonderful conversationalist and a woman of letters. Lewis was aglow in her presence.

Chapel

The **Chapel** (left), on the far right of the north wall of the First Court, was originally built in the 1470s and benefited from further restoration through the centuries. Lewis's rooms were located at the top of the Chapel Staircase, which is behind the screen just to the left of the Chapel door. Public access is not allowed to the staircase.

The Ante-chapel bears an understated plaque commemorating the presence of C. S. Lewis at Magdalene. It is located on the right wall as you enter the room. Lewis was a creature of routine and regularity. Attendance at chapel was a part of his orderly life. Lewis attended Morning Prayer (Matins) held at 8 a.m. He could be impatient and opinionated about how the services should be conducted. For example, Lewis strongly preferred said Evening Prayers to the sung service.

The favourite psalm of Lewis was Psalm 36 which reflects on light triumphing over darkness. Lewis perhaps remembered his introduction to the concept of a 'bright shadow' from George MacDonald's *Phantastes, a faerie Romance*. This sense of light on all things was a metaphor that enriched his life as one who was spiritually illumined and became an illuminator of text and thought. Also, Magdalen College in Oxford claimed Psalm 36:9 as the college scripture verse: 'For with thee is the well of life: and in thy light shall we see light.'

Verse one of the psalm spoke to Lewis more of his own depravity and sinfulness rather than the wanton state of others. The rich Ulster pronunciation of Lewis stood out in chapel services as he rolled off verses that were important to him:

> An oracle is within my heart concerning the
> sinfulness of the wicked:
> There is no fear of God before his eyes.
> Your love, O Lord, reaches to the heavens,
> Your faithfulness to the skies.

Your righteousness is like the mighty mountains,
your justice like the great deep.
Psalm 36: 1, 5, 6a (New International Version)

The seat habitually claimed by Lewis was the far back corner on the left side as you enter the intimate chapel. It was his custom to sit near the door of his parish church near Oxford to slip out as the service was ending. Perhaps he had the same thought in mind at Magdalene's Chapel (below).

Barrington-Ward recalled how Lewis would set his tea-kettle on the low-gas setting before coming to the chapel for morning prayers. For a concise service, the kettle, which could be heard in the chapel from his nearby rooms, would whistle after the service ended. However, if the prayers went on a bit longer than usual, the kettle, which would start with a low, soft whistle building to a shrill, urgent call, reminded all in the chapel that prayers had gone on too long. Lewis would slip out to rescue the kettle to signal that his time of prayer was over even if the service was not.

Widely recognized as a speaker, Lewis gathered quite an audience of devoted followers. More than a million people listened to his weekly fifteen-minute talks on Christianity broadcast on the BBC beginning in the early 1940s. Lewis's book **Mere Christianity** was a product of these talks. Frequently in demand as a preacher, Lewis presented his most famous sermon, 'The Weight of Glory' at Oxford University Church of St Mary the Virgin on 8 June 1941.

The last sermon ever preached by Lewis, 'A Slip of the Tongue', was delivered at a candlelit Sunday evensong in this chapel on 29 January 1956, at the invitation of the chaplain. The intimacy of the chapel was accentuated by the presence of more than a hundred people who claimed every possible space including the choir stalls. Folding chairs were brought to the chapel and many stood for the duration of the service.

The sermon title emerged from a slip of his tongue that occurred during an evening prayer when Lewis exchanged the word 'eternal' for 'temporal'. In his sermon Lewis addressed the human urge to focus on the temporal life instead of eternity.

Lewis slipped from this life on 22 November 1963, and was buried on 26 November 1963. His funeral was held at Holy Trinity, the Headington Quarry parish church outside Oxford, on a cold, sunny day with only a dozen people in attendance. His coffin was adorned with only a single candle, which burned confidently as the casket was carried from the church to the churchyard for burial.

A memorial service for Lewis was held in this chapel on Saturday, 7 December 1963. The service began with the words of Christ from John 11:25-26a: 'Jesus said to her, "I am the resurrection and the life. He who believes in me will live, even though he dies; and whoever lives and believes in me will never die."' A short reading from Lewis's sermon 'The Weight of Glory' that spoke of future glory, Christ the Morning Star, and the promise to the righteous to 'shine as the sun' concluded the simple service.

Hall (not open to public)

In the manner that was customary for university dons, Lewis took his meals in the Hall (below). Magdalene's Hall, an intimate setting, echoes vividly the original early sixteenth-century design. In 1714 the Hall was altered with the addition of a double staircase immediately to either side of the entry, which leads up to a small gallery. The Hall was never wired for electricity and to this day offers a candle-lit ambience for evening dining. The richly painted dark green and gold panelling showcases fifteen portraits of contributors to Magdalene's history including Samuel Pepys, Thomas Hardy and Rudyard Kipling.

There was one complaint about meals at Magdalene: Lewis lamented the fact that he could not eat breakfast until 8:30, delaying his letter writing until later. Because of his popularity as a writer, Lewis received a great deal of unsolicited fan mail, which he felt compelled to answer in addition to his other correspondence. This task fell entirely upon him in Cambridge, since his brother Warren was not present to relieve the burden from time to time as was the case in Oxford.

Lewis delighted in taking a challenge with his glass of wine at dinner. He liked the glass to be filled so that a meniscus formed above the rim. His ability to bring the glass to his lips without spilling a drop was his delight. Lewis would prove to have an entirely steady and successful hand even to the end of his days at Magdalene. While Lewis was content with a simple life, he did value good food and drink with ample friendship and conversation around the dinner table.

Combination Room (not open to public)

Traditionally, most of the Cambridge Halls would also have the Combination Room (common room) directly adjacent to the Hall. However, the original monastic design of the Hall and chapel did not lend itself to that configuration. Therefore, in 1712 the Combination Room (below) was added above the Old Kitchen and Buttery. The

elegant room boasts a fireplace, painted ceiling and stripped pine panelling. Opposite the fireplace is a stunning window, which highlights four coats of arms of people with ties with Magdalene.

Warnie, Jack's brother, remarked in a diary entry after Jack's move that his brother seemed happier and healthier at Cambridge. In Warren's estimation Oxford was characterized as hardboiled, materialistic, and scientific. He described how Cambridge was a more gentle, appealing environment where the majority of students and professors were 'Christian'.

Jack Lewis was much more a college man than a university one. He was intellectually enriched in the Anglican circle of twelve Magdalene fellows with whom he quickly felt comfortably at home in the more relaxed, friendly atmosphere. Each social occasion became an event under Lewis's charming, engaging glow.

The Combination Room in particular made an impression on Jack. After Hall, the dons would retire up the stairs to the candlelit Combination Room where the chairs were configured in a semicircle close to the fireplace in winter. As the days lengthened, the half circle arched at the other end of the room by the large windows that looked out into the First Court, allowing the men to bask in the final glow of daylight.

This was where the verbal battle of wit and intellect would commence. John Walsh, a junior don, found the addition of Lewis

> a force to be reckoned with. He flowered in Magdalene, which he found a far more congenial – and Christian – home than the more abrasive society of the other Magdalen, which he sharply depicted in *That Hideous Strength*. For a shy junior don, sitting in the candle-lit half circle of the Combination Room over coffee and port night after night, keeping one's conversational end up with Lewis was part ordeal, part delight, and certainly an education. He did not pick arguments, but if he did he liked to win them; in a debate with him I always felt at the wrong end of a Socratic dialogue. Lewis seemed not only to have read everything but to have remembered it as well; if one quoted – say – an obscure bit of Calvin, as likely as not he would continue or complete the quotation. He was the best-read man I have ever met, almost too well read…he would throw off lines of Euripides, not at all with the intention of displaying his learning, but in the simple, optimistic belief that everyone had ranged across European literature from Homer to Kipling as he had done.[12]

Lewis was in for one surprise, however, that marked a difference between his former and present college. When he learned that it was customary for the junior member to do the honours of pouring the port, Lewis enthusiastically assumed his task. However, when he took it upon himself to refill the glasses, he was gently told that Magdalene provided only one glass of port instead of Magdalen's customary three.

Pepys Library

As you enter the **Second Court**, you will see directly in front of you the Pepys Building (below) bearing the words *Bibliotheca Pepysiana 1724* indicating the year the Pepys collection was received by Magdalene

College. The library can be reached by taking the staircase just inside the far right archway. It is the one staircase that visitors are allowed to use at Magdalene.

The jewel of Magdalene is the library of Samuel Pepys. Pepys was born 23 February 1633, and died in 1703. He took up residence at Magdalene in 1651. During his years in Cambridge, Pepys completed a B.A. in 1654 and an M.A. in 1660. He was widely known as a civil servant, who chronicled a snapshot of London life in his notable diary from 1660 to 1669. Pepys contributed money to the building, which was completed sometime after 1700.

The library, which was donated to the college by his nephew after the death of Pepys, is precisely maintained according to the provisions of

Pepys's will. There are exactly 3,000 books that are not to be added to or taken from. Pepys firmly believed that a private library should reflect the interests of the owner and not be larger than what can be used.

The splendidly bound volumes are displayed in the twelve handsome oak bookcases (also known as 'presses') in a prescribed format ranging from the smallest book (numbered 1) to the largest book (numbered 3000). Many shelves have double rows of books on them: tall books to the back, small ones to the front. The librarian can readily access the books from the shelves with a charted table that catalogues their placement. Included in the Pepys Library are the six volumes of the diary and other items of interest related to Pepys.

Early in the 1960s, Magdalene College decided to publish the Pepys diary but questioned whether some rather delicate sections ought to be included. While Jack Lewis detested faculty meetings and seldom spoke, he did assume a firm stance on why the diary should be published in its unexpurgated entirety. In a letter written to his colleagues, Lewis builds his case on the basis of two arguments. First, from a prudential viewpoint, the college would be open to both ridicule and possible prosecution if the diary were altered. Second, Lewis suggested that from a moral viewpoint the act of publication would not solely generate the immoral acts suggested in the text. The case was made to publish the diary in its unexpurgated form.

Lewis had read the diary. He spoke with extensive knowledge and great insight about Samuel Pepys and his diary at the annual college birthday dinner celebrating Pepys held on 23 February 1961, in Magdalene's Hall. Yet, it was of profound interest to Lewis's good friend and colleague Richard Ladborough that apparently Lewis visited the treasure trove of the Pepys Library only once. That occasion occurred when some friends from Oxford visited Lewis and asked to see the collection of books.

This seeming contradiction was consistent with the attitude that Jack Lewis placed upon material things and places. George Watson, former Lewis student and Cambridge colleague, puts his finger squarely on the principle that governed much of the life of Lewis. C. S. Lewis seldom went out of his way for the world because he was

> seemingly self-sufficient, or as nearly so as a human being can be: he enjoyed company, that is, but you never felt he needed it. Like Tolkien, he never visited the United States. The world came to him. When you visited him in Cambridge, in his college room, he would greet you warmly and talk enthusiastically; but he had laid down his pen to do so, and you did not doubt he had lifted it again before you left the room.[13]

Lewis rarely read a newspaper; he relied on the presumption that if anything interesting occurred, people would eventually tell him about it. His military experience in France during World War I generated a fierce dislike of foreign travel. The occasion of his second foreign trip, which was to Greece, came at the urging of his wife, Joy, a few months before her death.

Visual aesthetics were also of little interest to him. After Joy's death, Lewis realized he did not even have a decent picture of his wife by which to remember her. Students who frequented Lewis's college rooms found a shabby atmosphere with no decoration except for a cheap print over the fireplace. When his masculine literary friends gathered at the Kilns, they were urged to scuff their tobacco ash into the worn carpet to avoid cleaning it up. The Kilns soon became nicknamed 'The Midden', an Old English term for dung heap.

The strength of the imaginative power of Jack Lewis did not move him to seek the pleasure of going to places or seeing sights. Text to Lewis was all important: making sentences was what he did all day. He memorized text. He equated text with life as evidenced in his final scene of **The Last Battle**. The book ends with earthly existence represented as merely the preface to the chapters of the grand story yet to come. His mind readily stored the keen images of worlds vividly captured during his forays into literature and language.

The notable exception to Lewis's lack of interest in experiencing sights was his love of walking in nature. Walking was a time when he relished beauty, thought seriously and meditated quietly while absorbing the charm and character of the countryside. While he enjoyed both walking and talking, Lewis normally did not mix the activities.

Therefore, for Lewis to know Samuel Pepys, the place to go to was Pepys' diary, not the Pepys Library. Nonetheless, most of us would find it worth the time to mount the staircase to the Pepys Library during visiting hours and reflect on the rich collection contained therein as indeed Lewis once did.

Fellows' Garden

As you leave the Pepys Library at the archways on the ground floor, turn to the right and follow the path into the **Fellows' Garden**.

This delightful garden was a favourite spot for C. S. Lewis to sit or walk before Matins. The Monk's Walk, which is along the north garden wall provided Lewis a peaceful path for prayer and meditation. The space is about the same size as that the monks would have known in 1428 as part of the original land parcel.

C. S. Lewis was invigorated by his first five years at Cambridge. He tackled his new position with newfound zest and increased energy. However, after Joy's death in 1960, Lewis was plagued with various health problems and his physical activity gradually declined. John Mole was a student who came to Magdalene in 1961, which was about a year after Joy's death. Mole's staircase was near Lewis's lodgings, and he recalled that Lewis was often confined to his rooms and

> seldom emerged except for return journeys to his house in Oxford, or to take a regular afternoon walk in the Fellows Garden where (on the occasions I saw him there) he would end up sitting under a tree and staring into space. A private grief. He seemed to me then a remote, rigorous figure of curious absence, the effigy of a great scholar glimpsed through an aura of loss and autumnal pathos. Apart from occasional courtesies on the staircase, we spoke only once – at a College garden party in my third year. I was about to take my finals, and he was quick to give advice. Never take risks in the exam room. Stick to what you have prepared. Always remember that digression will get you nowhere. Nervous, overwhelmed by all that I knew I didn't know, and by nature whimsically digressive, I nodded myself out of his presence as an elderly dog-collared acquaintance nodded himself in, agreed entirely that the advice was sound, and wished me good luck and goodbye.[14]

C. S. Lewis found himself in declining health in July 1963 and with reluctance resigned his position at Cambridge. He calmly prepared for the possibility of his coming death. In a final letter by Lewis to Sir Henry Willink, Master of Magdalene College, dated 25 October 1963, he acknowledges his acceptance of an Honorary Fellowship. References are made to Simon Barrington-Ward, the Dean of Chapel, and two other Honorary Fellows:

> The ghosts of the wicked old women in Pope 'haunt the places where their honour died.' I am more fortunate, for I

shall haunt the place whence the most valued of my honours came.

I am constantly with you in imagination. If in some twilit hour anyone sees a bald and bulky spectre in the Combination Room or the garden, don't get Simon to exorcise it, for it is a harmless wraith and means nothing but good.

If I loved you all less I should think much of being thus placed ('so were I equall'd with them in renown') besides Kipling and Eliot. But the closer and more domestic bond between Magdalene makes that side of it seem unimportant.[15]

Lewis died quietly at his home in Oxford, The Kilns, in the late afternoon of 22 November 1963, the same day as the assassination of John F. Kennedy.

C. S. Lewis and Cambridge

Lewis loved Cambridge and found it rather different from Oxford. On the surface, there were distinctions between the two towns. Cambridge was found to be quiet, gentle and a small place in a more rural setting with abundant walking paths. Oxford was industrialized, secular and snobbish. On a deeper level, Lewis felt much more at home in his new setting and would often turn up at Cambridge during his time between terms because he missed it and his colleagues. The heart of Cambridge offers wonderful walks along the city streets as well as along the backs of the colleges, which are delightfully arranged along the banks of the River Cam.

Lewis often was seen walking with rounded shoulders on his meditative, solitary walks. At other times he would share time occasionally with another friend. Wearing a battered, dirty felt hat, he would walk with his hands clasped behind his back or with a walking stick. Lewis often took walks to **Fen Ditton** (about two miles north-east of Cambridge) stopping at a pub along the way for conversation and refreshment.

Another scenic walk he enjoyed was to go south-west of Cambridge along the River Cam to arrive at the idyllic village of **Grantchester**, which is about two miles away. You would find the lovely stroll in the open meadows and the reward of tea and scones at **The Orchard Tea Garden** a memorable outing, especially in spring with the orchard in blossom.

The Pickerel

Retrace your steps to the **Magdalene Porter's Lodge** (left). Coming out of the Gatehouse of Magdalene College, look to your left across the street where you will see **The Pickerel** (below), a Tudor inn dating back to the sixteenth century.

While at Oxford, Lewis was famous for meeting with his literary group, The Inklings, at pubs such as the Eagle and Child (affectionately know as the Bird and Baby) or the Lamb and Flag, both located on St Giles Street, Oxford. These gatherings were occasions for writers like J. R. R. Tolkien to read works in progress – such as his *Lord of the Rings* – to glean constructive criticism.

In Cambridge, Lewis conveniently walked across Magdalene Street to the Pickerel Inn. Its dark-panelled, smoky atmosphere is not too different from that which Lewis would have experienced in his day. This is the pub that Lewis frequented for hearty conversation and drink.

As you leave **The Pickerel** to continue your walk into the heart of historic Cambridge, you will note in your exploration during your walk several bookshops with both new and second-hand volumes. You may find a book – particularly of English literature – to be a fitting token with which to remember both C. S. Lewis and your time in Cambridge.

As you continue to the right from **The Pickerel** along **Magdalene Street**, you will almost immediately find the **River Cam** and a bridge (left). Cambridge derived its name from this river and an ancient bridge. The first bridge on this site was erected in the 800s. The street becomes **Bridge Street** (below) at the **Cam River**. Today in nice weather the area is busy with punting rather than the river commerce of bygone days. If the weather and time permit, you could take a break for a 45-minute boat ride to see the backs of the colleges. Otherwise this walking tour will end at **Mill Lane**, which also has punting at **Mill Pool** (p31).

Another notable sight near the river as you move down **Bridge Street** is the **Round Church** (below) or the Church of the Holy Sepulchre, one of the few surviving circular structures in England. It dates back to the early twelfth century and is a worthwhile place to stop in terms of unique architecture. The church also is home to Christian Heritage, which provides resources to highlight the rich Christian history of Cambridge.

Opposite the Round Church take **St John's Street**, which will become **Trinity Street** and in a short distance **King's Parade**.

Along this walk you will pass several colleges that Lewis would have visited as he interacted with other Cambridge University colleagues. This is also the route from Magdalene College that Lewis would have followed as he walked to give his lectures at Cambridge University. The exact location of the Lecture Hall will be indicated later.

On the right as you progress up **St John's Street** is **St John's College** (left). Founded in 1511, this college was the vision of Lady Margaret Beaufort, the mother of Henry VII and grandmother of Henry VIII. St John's is the second largest college in Cambridge. Its beautiful setting and the recognizable Bridge of Sighs, visible from the Backs, make it an interesting stop.

Barbara Reynolds, who lectured in Italian literature, often watched Lewis from the window of her flat in St John's College as he came from Magdalene College and turned from Bridge Street onto St John's Street. She recalled a day when she stepped out of her front door and met Lewis. Reynold's six-year-old daughter was with her. Coincidently, the mother and daughter had just finished reading a passage from *The Lion, the Witch and the Wardrobe* together. The little girl was quite distraught about Edmund's plight and asked to go for a walk.

As Lewis stopped to talk with Reynolds and her daughter, he was informed of the reason for the stroll. The congenial Lewis chatted for a few minutes clad in 'a shabby grey-green overcoat, a battered felt hat, and he carried a knobbly walking stick. His large face was ruddy and cheerful, like a countryman's. No one would have taken him for an academic.' Raising his hat in gentlemanly courtesy to the little girl, Lewis moved on for his walk. Reynolds remarked, 'There, that is the very man who wrote the book we've just been reading.' Relieved, the girl replied to her mother, 'Well, he looks as though he'd make it come out all right.'[16]

The beautiful chapel at St John's is the setting for choral Evensong held during term from Tuesday to Saturday at 18:30. The college had among its well-known members the poet William Wordsworth and political reformer William Wilberforce, as well as many Nobel Prize winners and theologians. As you leave the gate of St John's, continue up **St John's Street** by turning right.

In just a very short distance, you will come to **Trinity College** (below) where Lewis delivered a lecture series. In the early 1930s, Lewis established his expertise in Medieval and Renaissance Literature. His Oxford University lecture series 'Prolegomena to Medieval Poetry' was extremely popular. Jack Lewis was introduced to Cambridge University formally in the Lent Term of 1939 when he was invited to be a visiting lecturer. Twice a week Lewis delivered his wealth of knowledge on 'Prolegomena to the Study of Renaissance Poetry'. This series of lectures was repeated back at Oxford University the following term and in the years to come.

During Easter Term in 1944, Lewis was again in Cambridge on four Wednesdays from late April to May when he delivered the Clark Lectures at the invitation of the Master of **Trinity College**. In the preface to Lewis's book ***English Literature in the Sixteenth Century Excluding Drama***, Lewis acknowledges that this important lecture series was the basis for his most scholarly book, Volume III in the ***Oxford History of English Literature***. The complete series consisted of twelve books.

The Volume III project was a demanding venture that took nine years for Lewis to complete. During this time Lewis claimed that he tried to read every book written in that century and to write an essay on every author. It is no wonder Lewis affectionately referred to his contribution as OHEL.

Trinity College is the largest and richest of the colleges, dating back to 1546. There are several noteworthy items about Trinity. Notice at the gate the rich tribute to English royalty and the out-of-place chair leg instead of sceptre in the hand of the college founder Henry VIII – thanks to the antics of student pranksters.

As you face the gate, note the bay window on the wall to the right. This window (right) is in the room where Sir Isaac Newton lived during his student days and where he penned his work *Principia Mathematica*. The apple tree on the lawn in front of the window is a descendant of the original apple tree at Newton's home.

Entering **Trinity College** at the Gatehouse and going past the Porter's Lodge, you will come into the Great Court. As you stand at the gate of Trinity College, you will see the spacious court. Looking to the

right, you will notice a large clock above Edward III's gate (left). This clock chimes in a male and female voice on each strike and provides the basis for the attempt to run around the Great Court (380 yards) in the time the clock strikes noon (24 chimes). The film *Chariots of Fire* featured this attempt; however, the scene was not filmed at this location.

A visit to the **Chapel** and the **Ante-chapel** to the right of the clock will further confirm the influence of Trinity graduates. Numerous plaques and statues of tribute honour Trinity graduates who have garnered more than thirty Nobel Prizes and exercised great influence in their chosen fields.

Among Trinity's members are Isaac Newton, Francis Bacon, George Herbert, W. Thackeray, A. A. Milne, Alfred Tennyson and Prince Charles. Lord Byron is said to have bathed in the fountain in the centre of the Great Court.

If time permits, make a brief visit to the famous **Wren Library** (open 12:00–14:00 Monday–Friday and 10:30–12:30 on Saturday). The library is reached by going through the opening on the west side of the Great

Court to Nevile's Court. You will see the **Wren Library** on the west of the court with the stairway to the library on the far right. The **Wren Library** is an architectural jewel designed by Sir Christopher Wren and houses literary treasures such as an eighth century copy of Paul's epistles and a leaf of the 1456 *Gutenberg Bible*. Works by A. A. Milne, John Milton, A. E. Housman, R. L. Stevenson and George Eliot as well as others are on display.

When you leave **Trinity College**, go right along **Trinity Street**. Across the street you will see the **Cambridge University Bookshop** on the corner of **Trinity Street** and **St Mary's Street**. The operations of the Cambridge University Press are primarily located on the southeast edge of the city.

This is the site (1 Trinity Street) of the oldest bookshop in England where since 1581 books have been continually sold on this corner. Founded in 1534, Cambridge University Press has the distinction of being the oldest printing and publishing house in the world as well as the oldest university press.[17] The shop carries books written by Professor Lewis during his Cambridge years. You will find a wealth of scholarship on the shelves of this shop if you have time to browse.

Across the street from the bookshop is the university church **Great St Mary's**. This was a church where Lewis worshipped on many occasions. There is a grand view of the city from the church's tower for

a modest fee.

Pause for a moment to take in the splendid spires of **King's College Chapel** (left), which is the centrepiece of Cambridge's city centre. This famous building was begun in 1446 and completed some eighty years later. The strong musical tradition of King's is known worldwide. If you have time, you may wish to visit the chapel, for a fee, or return later to attend Evensong at 17:30, for no charge. Admired by Lewis as a building that he thought 'beautiful beyond hope or belief', the Chapel is one of the most striking buildings in the world.

One little detour you might wish to make at this time is to seek out the little alleyway almost directly across from King's College Chapel called **St Edward's Passage**. You will find several gems to visit here. As you go up the passage, you will see two bookshops that may be of interest to

you. On the right is **The Haunted Bookshop** that has a grand collection of used children's books. From the same spot to the left, you will also see **G. David** (left), a shop which carries a good selection of used and rare books and prints. It was a favourite stop for Lewis when he was out walking about town.

Lewis was a firm believer in frequenting second-hand bookshops to build his personal library. He was quick to urge his students to do likewise. From his excellent memory, Lewis would recite lists of classic works that *should* be on his students' shelves.

If **St Edward's Church** in the centre of this little courtyard happens to be open, you will see the pulpit where Hugh Latimer preached in this church that was used by the early Reformers in Cambridge. Time and weather permitting, you might stop just behind St Edward's Church to browse at **Market Hill** where there is a variety of goods and produce for sale on the open market stalls.

Mill Lane

As you continue, retrace your steps to **King's Parade**. The street will once again change names to **Trumpington Street**. At **Mill Lane** turn right and just a short distance down the street on the left you will see **8 Mill Lane**, the site of the **Cambridge University Lecture Rooms**. Today, the more recent Sidgwick Site is where most lectures take place.

Lewis, however, gave his lectures, including the guest lectures of his pre-Cambridge days, in this building. He would be seen several times a week walking from Magdalene College to Bridge Street and turning onto St John's Street until it turned into Trumpington Street. Usually he wore his academic gown but not the mortarboard, preferring a brimmed country-style hat that he wore when walking outdoors.

In the first years that Lewis was in Cambridge, the walk was easy. The last few years, however, friends could see the exhausting effort needed to make the walk. They often wished that Lewis would save his energy by taking a taxi.

Room 3, the largest room, was the setting of Professor Lewis's Inaugural Lecture, which was delivered at 5 p.m. on Monday, 29 November 1954, prior to his official move to Cambridge in January, 1955. The Inaugural Lecture was notable for several reasons. First, it was Lewis's fifty-sixth birthday. Secondly, the audience was exceedingly large. In addition to Cambridge academics, the event was supported by a large group from Oxford in attendance including his new friend Joy Davidman.

The large lecture room on Mill Lane was so crowded that the Oxonian group could find no place to sit except on the dais, surrounding Lewis, as a friend commented, like a wall of shields defending a liege lord. In fact, it was so crowded that the audience could not take notes.

Barbara Reynolds, who attended the occasion, recalled an audience where latecomers were seated on the floor. She remarked to friends that it was impossible to raise her elbow to take notes. Those in attendance agreed that it was a highly successful undertaking on Lewis's part. Lewis was introduced by Vice-Chancellor Willink, who mentioned 'that the unanimous eagerness with which the electors had invited Lewis to come to Cambridge was probably unique among such events.'[18]

The Inaugural Lecture entitled, *De Descriptione Temporum* did as the title suggested: Lewis expanded 'on describing the times'. Even the choice of the lecture's title directed the audience to the tone of the event for

> Lewis chose a Latin title to emphasize his bookish and clerkly cast of mind, as a medieval and Renaissance scholar operating within an unbookish post-Christian culture. After discussing the claims of the fall of Rome, the

Renaissance, and the Reformation, he concludes that the Industrial Revolution marked the 'Great Divide' between the ancient and modern civilization.[19]

Lewis characterized himself as an 'Old Western Man' and a dinosaur. Even his known archaic lifestyle suggested he belonged to another age. He shunned the media. The only exceptions were when he listened to his own BBC radio broadcasts to critique himself or when he picked up a newspaper to amuse himself with a crossword puzzle. He hated machines and never learned to drive or to use a typewriter. His Oxford colleagues had long regarded Lewis as an old fashioned, obsolete champion of the past.

Yet, Lewis challenged with wit: if a dinosaur would drag its immense body into a laboratory, would not the frightened, fleeing audience look back over their shoulders at this curious specimen? He invited his audience to consider his literary convictions before he became extinct. No doubt Lewis was referring to the tension that existed between his bias and modern literary criticism.

The European literary approach embraced by Lewis was based upon using the Bible and the Classics as a foundation; he was a lover of books and words who immersed himself in the text. The recent practice of reading scholarly commentaries as well as lacking sufficient Classical background was in his opinion a dangerous literary habit.

Magdalene College colleague John Stevens explains

if talk was his play, books were his love. The enthusiasm and relish which C.S.L. brought to his reading, and that not only in the fields where he was acknowledged master, were infectious. He did not regard himself as a scholar, but as a man of letters. The backgrounds of academic controversy, research and criticism were kept rigorously in their place. He spent his time reading texts rather than reading about them.[20]

The lecture was declared by Joy Davidman to be 'funny as hell...there were so many capped and gowned dons in the front rows that they looked like a rookery'.[21] Others described the lecture as being brilliant, intellectual, exciting and humorous.

The audience warmly received the extemporaneous delivery of Lewis in which he hardly referred to his notes. However, many were also initially disappointed. His lack of notes seemed a tragic oversight, which would prevent the publication of a text, as was the usual tradition. Therefore, it was even more thrilling to find the word-for-word lecture published almost immediately by Cambridge University Press. The lecture gave testimony to Lewis's amazing memory since experienced lecturers in the audience had assumed it was an improvised talk.

Lewis was hugely popular as a lecturer and would often have a great audience when he delivered his lectures at Mill Lane. A lecture hall was a public theatre where his gifts were most aptly showcased. He assumed an authoritative stance with a commanding presence. Lewis used a magical thread of masterful imagination to weave together lectures intertwined with vivid images to bind his audience's attention. Lewis held his audience captive as he cast a spell with his remarkably clear exposition of the most complex ideas and his evident range of rhetorical ability.

His rich, resonant voice gave the distinct impression that he was speaking to just one other person; he gave the same impression in his radio addresses. The vocal quality of Lewis was consistent; he had a rich voice that pointed to his Ulster roots with its rolled *rs*. His velvety voice filled the lecture hall with a loud voice (as opposed to the characteristic academic lectures that were soft and slow) that catered for students who took notes.

The lecture was precisely organized in a segmented outline format with main sections and subsections. Lewis firmly believed that ideas should be 'tidied up to look like a salad rather than a stew. He hated mishmash...He thought ideas should have space around them to breathe.'[22]

The gift of clarity was evidenced by his rich usage of illustrations, analogies and quotations. Lewis possessed eloquence in his word choice, yet was never intellectually snobbish. His chauffeur Clifford Morris testified that Lewis used him as a sounding board. If an idea were not understandable to Morris, Lewis would often abandon the original idea and start over again.

He often organized his lecture notes in a notebook with the left-hand page containing the actual lecture outline and the right-hand page

33

supporting the material with quotations and specific instances neatly organized and concisely penned with his steel pen nib. These notebooks of lectures were the basis for many of Lewis's academic books.

The final nine years of C. S. Lewis's life as a Cambridge professor were years that reflected the happiness of his married life, the depths of grief after the death of his wife, and the adjustment to ageing and declining health. They were also academically productive years that included the publication of thirteen books, numerous poems, short stories, book reviews and forty-four articles. About one million paperback copies of his books were sold by the year he died.

For decades readers have marvelled at the breadth and depth of C. S. Lewis's literary repertoire. He has regaled children at heart with *The Chronicles of Narnia*, revealed literary scholarship in *English Literature in the Sixteenth Century*, proclaimed essential theological beliefs in *Mere Christianity*, carried imaginations from heaven to hell in *Screwtape Letters*, and revealed his personal journey in *Surprised by Joy*. Lewis left the world the gifts of his intellect, story, spiritual thought and imagination that ever endear him to the hearts of audiences young and old.

And we have the word of the prophets made more certain,
and you will do well to pay attention to it, as to
a light shining in a dark place, until the day dawns
and the morning star rises in your hearts.

2 Peter 1:19 (New International Version)

Endnotes

1 Nevill Coghill in *Light on C. S. Lewis*, ed. Jocelyn Gibb, 1965, p. 63.

2 According to the *Oxford English Dictionary*, both spellings Madgalen and Magdalene are acceptable. The vernacular form of the word is Maudlin (modlin) represented by the pronunciation currently still in use for both Magdalen College, Oxford, and Magdalene College, Cambridge. The name Magdalen(e) is supposed to be identical with the unnamed sinner in Luke 7:35 – a harlot restored to purity and elevated to sainthood by repentance and faith; a reformed prostitute. Lewis contrasts his early life as an avowed atheist with the change that came to his life transformed by the Lord through repentance and faith.

3 From a collection of letters between Lewis, Sir Henry Willink, and the Electors (including J. R. R. Tolkien) over Lewis's election from the Magdalene College Archives, Group F, Private Papers. Lewis's move to Cambridge is summarized in an article entitled, 'C. S. Lewis: From Magdalen to Magdalene', *Magdalene College Magazine and Record*, 32, (1988), pp. 42-46. Reprinted in *Critical Essays on C. S. Lewis (Critical Thought Series: I)*, ed. George Watson (Aldershot; Scholar Press, 1992).

4 *Ibid.*

5 Group F, Private Papers, Magdalene College Archives containing correspondence documenting the unfolding of Lewis's acceptance of the Chair of Medieval and Renaissance English.

6 William Griffin, *Clive Staples Lewis: A Dramatic Life*, 1986, p. 356.

7 John Walsh, 'Reminiscences – Magdalene, 1948-1958,' *Magdalene College Magazine and Record*, 34 (1989-90), pp. 45-49.

8 Group F, Private Papers, Magdalene College Archives.

9 Derek Brewer, 'The Tutor: A Portrait', in *C. S. Lewis at the Breakfast Table*, ed. James Como. 1992, chapter 6.

10 Excerpt from a sermon delivered by Rt. Revd. Simon Barrington-Ward in Magdalene College Chapel on 11 October 1998.

11 Walter Hooper, *C. S. Lewis: A Companion and Guide*, 1996, p. 42.

12 Walsh, pp. 45-49.

13 George Watson, 'The Art of Disagreement: C.S. Lewis (1898-1963)', *Hudson Review*, 48 (Summer 1995), pp. 234-236.

14 John Mole, 'Reminiscences', *Magdalene College Magazine and Record*, 32, (1987-88), pp. 47-48.

15 Group F. Private Papers, Magdalene College Archives.

16 Barbara Reynolds, 'Memories of C. S. Lewis in Cambridge', *Chesterton Review*, XVII, Nos. 3,4 (August, November 1991), pp. 380-381.

17 Michael Black, *A Short History of Cambridge University Press, 2000*, pp. 1, 59.

18 Barbara Reynolds, pp. 378-384.

19 Lionel Adey, *C.S. Lewis: Writer, Dreamer, and Mentor*, 1998, p. 238.

20 John E. Stevens, 'In Memoriam: Professor C. S. Lewis', *Magdalene College Magazine and Record*, 8, (1963-1964), p. 13.

21 Hooper, pp. 72-73.

22 Watson, pp. 235-236.

Selected Bibliography

Adey, Lionel. *C. S. Lewis: Writer, Dreamer, and Mentor.* Cambridge, UK: Eerdmans, 1998.

Como, James T., editor. *C. S. Lewis at the Breakfast Table and Other Reminiscences.* New York: Harvest Book, 1992.

Gibb, Jocelyn, editor. *Light on C. S. Lewis.* New York: Harvest, 1965.

Gibson, Evan K. *C. S. Lewis, Spinner of Tales: A Guide to His Fiction.* Grand Rapids, MI: Eerdmans, 1973.

Green, Roger Lancelyn & Hooper, Walter. *C. S. Lewis : A Biography.* London: Collins, 1974.

Gresham, Douglas. *Lenten Lands: My Childhood with Joy Davidman and C. S. Lewis.* New York: Macmillan, 1985.

Griffin, William. *Clive Staples Lewis: A Dramatic Life.* New York: Harper and Row, 1986.

Hooper, Walter. *C. S. Lewis: A Companion and Guide.* London: Fount, 1996.

Lewis, C. S. *Surprised by Joy.* London: Harvest Book, 1955.

Sayer, George. *Jack: A Biography.* Wheaton, IL: Crossway, 1994.

Sibley, Brian. *Shadowlands: The Story of C. S. Lewis and Joy Davidman.* London: Hodder and Stoughton, 1985.

Schultz, Jeffrey & West, John, editors. *The C. S. Lewis Reader's Encyclopedia.* Grand Rapids: Zondervan, 1998.

Suggested Clive Staples Lewis Reading List

The Chronicles of Narnia
A Grief Observed
Mere Christianity
Screwtape Letters
Surprised by Joy
Till We Have Faces
Weight of Glory

Special thanks to the Master and Fellows of Magdalene College